I love you to the moon & back!

# Prayers for your Child from Head to Toe

Shartia LOVE Jones

Love, Shartia

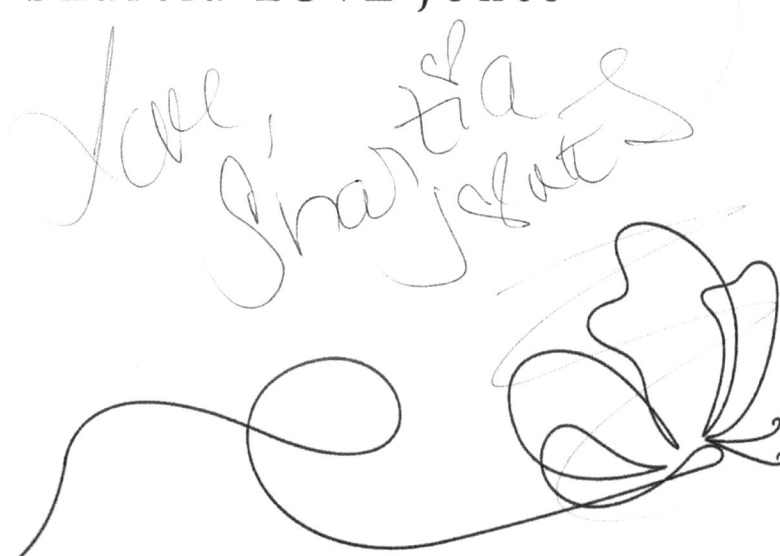

S.H.E. PUBLISHING, LLC

Prayers for Your Child ; from head to toe.
Copyright © 2022 by Shartia Love Jones.

All rights reserved. Printed in the United States of America. No part of this booklet may be used or reproduced in any manner whatsoever without written permission except in the case of brief quotations embodied in critical articles or reviews.

For information contact :
**www.shepublishingllc.com**
**info@shepublishingllc.com**

Book Cover and Title Page design by Michelle Phillips of
CHELLD3 3D VISUALIZATION AND DESIGN

ISBN: 978-1-953163-48-6

First Edition : August 2022

10 9 8 7 6 5 4 3 2 1

# DEDICATION

This book is dedicated to God, who has made all this possible. I also would like to dedicate it to my son, James Tate III. You are a true joy! My life is filled with so much love and adoration with you by my side. I learn from you daily. You are loved beyond words and actions. I want you to always believe in yourself, love exactly who you are and always be willing to grow and expand. You are intelligent, kind, handsome and mannerable. There aren't many like you, be proud of this son for this is the way God has called us to be! I thank God for you every day and I want you to thank HIM too! Continue to be great! Always remember that even when times and people seem to go low, you always have a choice to go and look up high! When things and people change, know that God remains the same. That is where your help will come from, God.

To all the parents and caregivers who would like to pray over their children and would like a little guidance, I also share this dedication with you. Becoming a parent can be a fearful and worrisome thing. However, if we give our concerns to the Lord, we will not have to worry anymore. Let's pray for our children.

I also dedicate this book to my praying, consistent, God-fearing, and Beautiful Grandmother Florence Watkins. I would have been taken out long ago if it were not for her. I'm sure that the prayers she's prayed, my ancestors prayed; the blood, sweat, and tears are not in vain. My grandmother reminds me that God is our source. He is our reason for everything and is our help in our time of need. This has been the communication that has left her lips since I can recall. As I get older, I understand the importance and live in this truth. My Grandma is very humble, but know that I know God, seek God's presence and love God because of the Love she shared with me regarding our God. My paternal Grandma, Adeline Elizabeth Charley-Jones is in Heaven already, and I thank God for her too. I am certain she is up there praying and dispatching angels on our behalf. I love both of my Grandmothers, and I thank God for giving me the ear to listen and the heart to understand... I am still a work in progress, but I am forever seeking the wisdom of God. I love you, Lil Mama, and your prayers, our talks, and our spiritual discussions bless me beyond measure. To God be the Glory. I miss both of my Grandfathers; Blanche Jones Sr. and Floyd C. Watkins... I love you both very much. Thank you for being our angels, I know you two are watching over us.

# CONTENTS

**INTRODUCTION** ............................................................................. i

**The Head** ........................................................................................ 1

*Luke 12:7 (NIV) | Indeed, the very hairs of your head are all numbered. Do not fear; you are more valuable than many sparrows.*

**The Eyes** ......................................................................................... 6

*Psalm 17:8 (NIV) | Keep me as the apple of the eye; hide me under the shadow of thy wings.*

**The Ears** ........................................................................................ 11

*Romans 10:17 (KJV) | So then faith cometh by hearing, and hearing by the word of God.*

**The Nose** ....................................................................................... 16

*Genesis 2:7 (NIV) | Then the Lord formed man of dust from the ground, and breathed into his nostrils the breath of life, and man became a living being.*

**The Mouth** .................................................................................... 21

*Proverbs 15:4 (KJV) | A wholesome tongue is a tree of life: but perverseness therein is a breach in the spirit.*

**The Neck** ....................................................................................... 27

*Job 41:22 (KJV) | In his neck remaineth strength, and sorrow is turned into joy before him.*

### The Shoulder      32

*Deuteronomy 33:12 (KJV) | And of Benjamin he said, The beloved of the Lord shall dwell in safety by him; And the Lord shall cover him all the day long, And he shall dwell between his shoulders.*

### The Back/Spine      38

*Exodus 1:9 (NIV) | The Lord will fight for you, you need only be still.*

### The Hands      43

*Psalm 24:4-5 (KJV) | He that hath clean hands, and a pure heart; who hath not lifted up his soul, unto vanity nor sworn deceitfully. He shall receive the blessing from the God of his salvation*

### The Arms      49

*Mark 10:16 (KJV) | And he took them up in his arms, put his hands upon them, and blessed them.*

### The Belly      54

*Job 40:16 (KJV) | Lo now, his strength is in his loins, and his force is in the navel of his belly.*

### The Heart      60

*Matthew 5:8 (KJV) | Blessed are the pure in heart: for they shall see God.*

### The Private & Sacred Area      66

*1 Timothy 5:22 (KJV) | Lay hands suddenly on no man, neither be partaker of other men's sins: keep thyself pure.*

**The Legs**                                                                                   **72**

*Song of Solomon 5:15 (KJV)| His legs are as pillars of marble, set upon sockets of fine gold: his countenance is as Lebanon, excellent as the cedars.*

**The Knees**                                                                           **78**

*Luke 11:1 (KJV)| And it came to pass, that, as he was praying in a certain place, when he ceased, 1 of his disciples said until him Lord teach us to pray as John also taught his disciples.*

**The Feet**                                                                               **83**

*2 Samuel 22:37 (KJV)| Thou hast enlarged my steps under me; so that my feet did not slip.*

**You**                                                                                     **88**

*Malachi 4:2 (KJV)| But unto you that fear my name shall the Sun of righteousness arise with healing in his wings; and ye shall go forth, and grow up as calves of the stall*

# INTRODUCTION

**W**elcome! Whether you are a new parent/guardian, a soon-to-be parent/guardian, or anyone else who would like to strengthen your prayer life as it pertains to children... I invite you to this prayer experience. I know I had troubled thoughts at times while raising our son. In order to help you with your prayers, concerns, and maybe your worries, please feel free to write. I want this book to be one you reference as often as needed. Your thoughts and feedback are appreciated, desired, and welcomed!

When you see "insert a picture of your child's head," be sure to go and get a picture or take a picture of that specific body part to paste into the book. I invite you to treat your additions to this book as a safe space. A space for you to share your intimate thoughts, prayers, etc. When the book calls for you to write your specific prayer, be sure to speak from the heart. There is no such thing as a "Perfect Prayer." God hears all things. Next, when you get to the "Reflection and Feeling" section, write down any feelings or thoughts that come to mind as you read the gratitude section, prayer, and scriptures. Being honest with yourself is of utmost importance, and there are no right or wrong answers. As your prayers are being answered, I want you to enjoy these moments. However, it is important that we recall when our prayers are answered! This is why you will find a section called Gratitude and Acknowledgement.

I honestly want you to feel free to write in this book wherever you feel the need to do so. (You can highlight as well). Lastly, you will be invited to write your overall thoughts at the end of the book. Take time and live in the moment as you write. Again, I want this book to be a "go-to" and a true resource for you. Trust and believe in your written thoughts. Finally, please enjoy the Morning and Bedtime Prayers I have included for your prayer pleasure on the next page. Thank you for your purchase. Thank you for believing in me, thank you for believing in your efforts, and most importantly, thank you for trusting God.

A Prayer Book for My Child(ren)

iii | Prayers for Your Child; from Head to Toe

## Prayer for Morning

**(Wake up Prayer)**

Now I'm awake from my sleep,

I thank you Lord for keeping me.

Please keep safe and guide my day,

I love you Lord in every way!!!

Amen!

**A Prayer Book for My Child(ren)**

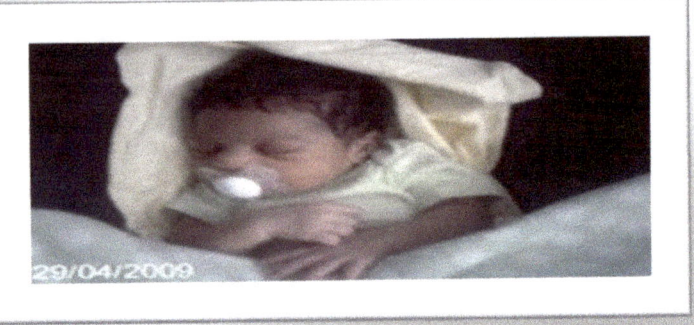

# Prayer for Bedtime

Now I lay me down to sleep,

I pray the Lord my soul to keep,

Please Keep me safe while I rest,

I love you Lord, You're the BEST!!!

Amen!

**A Prayer Book for My Child(ren)**

**A Prayer Book for My Child(ren)**

# The Head

Luke 12:7 (NIV)| Indeed, the very hairs of your head are all numbered. Do not fear; you are more valuable than many sparrows.

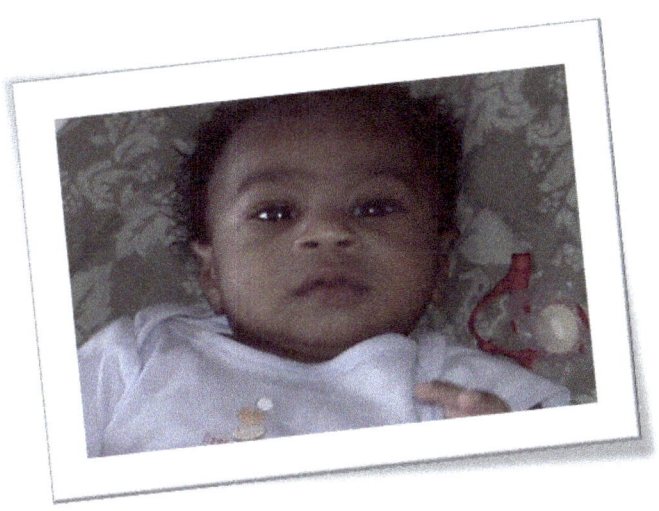

Lord, we thank you for giving our child a brain. We pray that he/she can gain wisdom, think independently, acknowledge You, and develop appropriately. We also pray that You will bless and physically and mentally protect our child's head. Our son has a wealth of thoughts, wishes, dreams, and intelligence. If our child has health challenges with their head, we pray for the miracle of healing. Lord, please touch (or adorn) our babies' head and call it blessed.

*Wisdom is the principal thing; therefore, get wisdom: and with all thy getting, get understanding.* **Proverbs 4:7 (KJV)**

*But grow in grace, and in the knowledge of our Lord and Saviour Jesus Christ. To him be glory both now and forever. Amen.*
**Peter 3:18 (NIV)**

---

**We pray the Lord will bless and protect our child's head. Thank you, Lord, for blessing and protecting our child's head.**

---

Insert a Picture of _____ head ☺
(Insert your child's name)

A Prayer Book for My Child(ren)

# 3 | Prayers for Your Child; from Head to Toe

> **This is your "Safe Space."**
> **Feel free to express yourself.**

*In this moment:*

What are your present thoughts, feelings, and emotions?

_____
_____
_____
_____
_____
_____
_____
_____
_____
_____
_____
_____
_____
_____
_____
_____

**A Prayer Book for My Child(ren)**

*In this moment:*

Write your personal prayer for your child(ren):

_____
_____
_____
_____
_____
_____
_____
_____
_____
_____
_____
_____
_____
_____
_____
_____
_____
_____
_____
_____

**A Prayer Book for My Child(ren)**

## Gratitude and Acknowledgement:

Please write your reflections on your answered personal prayer:

# The Eyes

Psalm 17:8 (NIV) | Keep me as the apple of the eye; hide me under the shadow of thy wings.

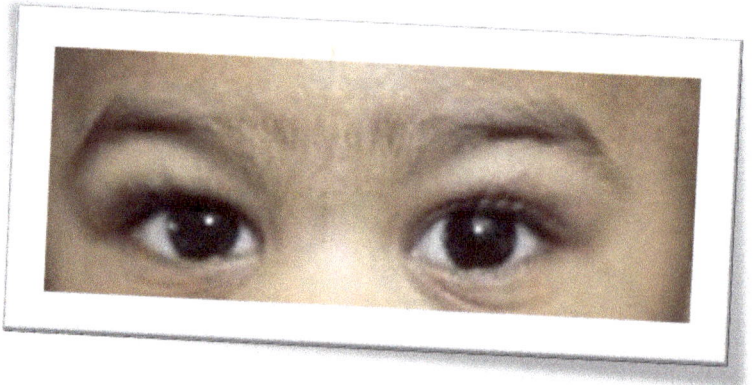

A Prayer Book for My Child(ren)

Lord, we thank you for giving our child a pair of healthy eyes. We thank You for allowing our child to have a sense of sight. If your child has health challenges with their eyes, we pray for the miracle of healing. Lord, we pray our child will seek You and Your wisdom daily. We also pray you will allow our child to see and experience wonderful things, colors, and the many wonders of Your beautiful world.

We pray You protect their eyes from what You want to shield them from. Please keep their eyes healthy, bright, and focused on You. Lord, please touch our child's eyes and call them blessed.

*But seek ye first the kingdom of God, and his righteousness; and all these things shall be added unto you.* **Matthew 6:33 (KJV)**

*Keep my commandments, and live; and my law as the apple of thine eye.* **Proverbs 7:2 (KJV)**

> **We pray the Lord will bless and protect our child's eyes.**

Insert a Picture of _____ eyes ☺
(Insert your child's name)

> This is your "Safe Space."
> Feel free to express yourself.

## In this moment:

What are your present thoughts, feelings, and emotions?

_____
_____
_____
_____
_____
_____
_____
_____
_____
_____
_____
_____
_____
_____
_____
_____
_____
_____
_____

## In this moment:

Write your personal prayer for your child(ren):

_____
_____
_____
_____
_____
_____
_____
_____
_____
_____
_____
_____
_____
_____
_____
_____
_____
_____
_____
_____

## Gratitude and Acknowledgement:

Please write your reflections on your answered personal prayer:

_____
_____
_____
_____
_____
_____
_____
_____
_____
_____
_____
_____
_____
_____
_____
_____
_____
_____
_____
_____
_____
_____
_____
_____

# The Ears

Romans 10:17 (KJV) | So then faith cometh by hearing, and hearing by the word of God.

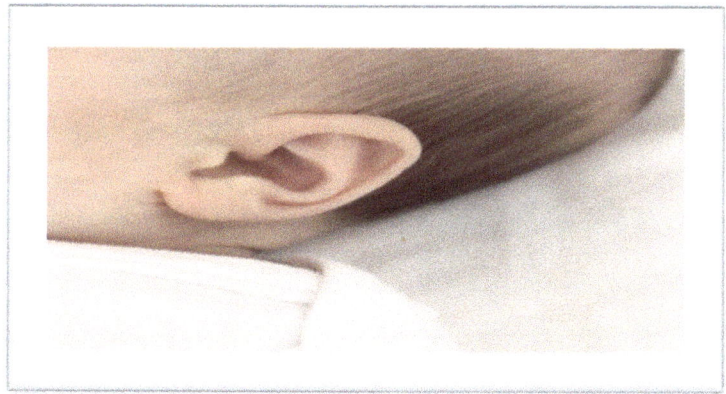

Lord, we thank you for allowing our child to have the sense of hearing. Lord, we pray that our child will have faith, which comes from hearing. We also pray he/she will listen to their parents, grandparents, teachers, true friends, spiritual teachers, God-Parents, and family. Please allow our child(ren) to hear well and to have a high level of discernment. We also pray they listen and learn at the developmentally appointed times. Please keep their ears clear of ear infections and other ear illnesses. If your child has health challenges with their ears, we pray for the miracle of healing. Lastly, we pray that you will allow our child(ren) to listen and learn Your will and Your way throughout their lives.

*Children, obey your parents in all things; for this is well pleasing unto the Lord.* **Colossians (3:20)**

**We pray the Lord will bless and protect our child's ears.**

Insert a Picture of _____ ears ☺
(Insert your child's name)

> This is your "Safe Space."
> Feel free to express yourself.

## *In this moment:*

What are your present thoughts, feelings, and emotions?

_____
_____
_____
_____
_____
_____
_____
_____
_____
_____
_____
_____
_____
_____
_____
_____
_____

## *In this moment:*

Write your personal prayer for your child(ren):

_____
_____
_____
_____
_____
_____
_____
_____
_____
_____
_____
_____
_____
_____
_____
_____
_____
_____
_____
_____
_____

## Gratitude and Acknowledgement:

Please write your reflections on your answered personal prayer:

_____
_____
_____
_____
_____
_____
_____
_____
_____
_____
_____
_____
_____
_____
_____
_____
_____
_____
_____

# The Nose

Genesis 2:7 (NIV) | Then the Lord formed man of dust from the ground, and breathed into his nostrils the breath of life, and man became a living being.

Lord, we thank you for allowing our child to have the sense of smell. Lord, we pray for our child's nose, which is directly connected to his/her sense of taste. Please protect their nasal passages and keep them from dealing with extreme colds, Covid-19, allergies, severe nosebleeds, bronchial/sinus infections (*and if the child must experience these illnesses, please allow healing to occur throughout*). If your child has health challenges with their nose/breathing, we pray for miracles and that they will be healed soon.

*But I have all, and abound: I am full, having received of Epaphroditus the things which were sent from you, an odor of a sweet smell, a sacrifice acceptable, well pleasing to God.* **Philippians 4:18 (KJV)**

**We pray the Lord will bless and protect our child's nose.**

Insert a Picture of _____ nose ☺
(Insert your child's name)

> **This is your "Safe Space."**
> **Feel free to express yourself.**

# In this moment:

What are your present thoughts, feelings, and emotions?

_____
_____
_____
_____
_____
_____
_____
_____
_____
_____
_____
_____
_____
_____
_____
_____
_____
_____
_____

## In this moment:

Write your personal prayer for your child(ren):

_____

_____

_____

_____

_____

_____

_____

_____

_____

_____

_____

_____

_____

_____

_____

_____

_____

_____

_____

## Gratitude and Acknowledgement:

Please write your reflections on your answered personal prayer:

_____

_____

_____

_____

_____

_____

_____

_____

_____

_____

_____

_____

_____

_____

_____

_____

_____

# The Mouth

Proverbs 15:4 (KJV) | A wholesome tongue is a tree of life: but perverseness therein is a breach in the spirit.

Lord, we thank you for allowing our child to have the sense of taste and the ability to talk. If our child does not have use of this sense... We pray for miracles and that they will be speaking soon. Lord, please help my child know what to say, when to say it, and when to hold their tongue in the same respect.

Lord, we pray that our child will speak good things; we pray for the filter over our child's mouth regardless of what the peers may be saying or doing. We also pray they will be health conscious about their food and beverage consumption. Lord, we pray they will speak highly of You and share Your stories of the bible and testimonies with the world. We pray our child practices self-advocacy. If your child has health challenges with their mouth/throat/etc., we pray for miracles and that they will be healed soon.

*Death and life are in the power of the tongue: and they that love it shall eat the fruit thereof.* **Proverbs 18:21 (KJV)**

*If ye be willing and obedient, ye shall eat the good of the land.* **Isaiah 1:19 (KJV)**

*And also that every man should eat and drink, and enjoy the good of all his labour, it is the gift of God.*
**Ecclesiastes 3:1 (KJV)**

> **We pray the Lord will bless, protect and hold our child's mouth.**

A Prayer Book for My Child(ren)

Insert a Picture of _____ mouth ☺
(Insert your child's name)

**A Prayer Book for My Child(ren)**

> **This is your "Safe Space."**
> **Feel free to express yourself.**

# In this moment:

What are your present thoughts, feelings, and emotions?

_____
_____
_____
_____
_____
_____
_____
_____
_____
_____
_____
_____
_____
_____
_____
_____
_____

# In this moment:

Write your personal prayer for your child(ren):

_____

_____

_____

_____

_____

_____

_____

_____

_____

_____

_____

_____

_____

_____

_____

_____

_____

_____

_____

## Gratitude and Acknowledgement:

Please write your reflections on your answered personal prayer:

_____

_____

_____

_____

_____

_____

_____

_____

_____

_____

_____

_____

_____

_____

_____

_____

_____

# The Neck

Job 41:22 (KJV) | In his neck remaineth strength, and sorrow is turned into joy before him.

Lord, we thank you for blessing our child with a strong neck to help align their body accordingly. If your child has health challenges with their neck area, we pray for miracles and that they will be healed soon.

Lord, we pray You continue to strengthen his/her neck so they keep their head held high and remain positive in life. We also pray You will lift some of the burdens off their shoulders as You grant them grace and mercy.

*So shall they be life unto thy soul, and grace to thy neck.*
**Proverbs 3:22 (KJV)**

*And it shall come to pass in that day, that his burden shall be taken away from off thy shoulder, and his yoke from off thy neck, and he yoke shall be destroyed because of the anointing.*
**Isaiah 10:27 (KJV)**

**We pray the Lord will bless and protect our child's neck.**

Insert a Picture of _____ neck ☺
(Insert your child's name)

A Prayer Book for My Child(ren)

> **This is your "Safe Space."**
> **Feel free to express yourself.**

## In this moment:

What are your present thoughts, feelings, and emotions?

_____
_____
_____
_____
_____
_____
_____
_____
_____
_____
_____
_____
_____
_____
_____
_____
_____

## In this moment:

Write your personal prayer for your child(ren):

_____
_____
_____
_____
_____
_____
_____
_____
_____
_____
_____
_____
_____
_____
_____
_____
_____

## Gratitude and Acknowledgement:

Please write your reflections on your answered personal prayer:

_____
_____
_____
_____
_____
_____
_____
_____
_____
_____
_____
_____
_____
_____
_____
_____
_____
_____
_____
_____

# The Shoulder

Deuteronomy 33:12 (KJV) | And of Benjamin he said, The beloved of the Lord shall dwell in safety by him; And the Lord shall cover him all the day long, And he shall dwell between his shoulders.

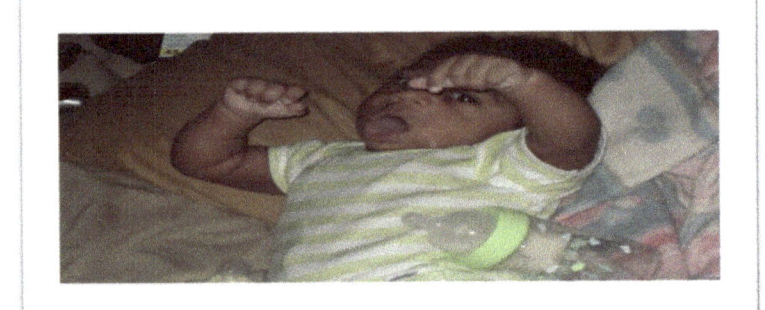

Lord, we thank You for blessing our child with shoulders that help to align his/her body accordingly.

Lord, we pray You continue to square out our child's shoulders, so they head in the right direction in life. We also pray you will lift some of the burdens off our child's shoulders as You grant grace and mercy, and apply the weight of Your lessons when You see fit. We pray he/she can deal with life's ups and downs and will remain optimistic. If your child has health challenges with their shoulders, we pray for miracles and that they will be healed soon.

*That I will break the Assyrian in my land, and upon my mountains tread him under foot: then shall his yoke depart off them, and his burden depart from off their shoulders.* **Isaiah 14:25 (KJV)**

> **We pray the Lord will bless, protect, and guide our child's shoulders.**

Insert a Picture of _____ shoulders ☺
(Insert your child's name)

**A Prayer Book for My Child(ren)**

> This is your "Safe Space."
> Feel free to express yourself.

## *In this moment:*

What are your present thoughts, feelings, and emotions?

_____
_____
_____
_____
_____
_____
_____
_____
_____
_____
_____
_____
_____
_____
_____
_____
_____
_____

*In this moment:*

Write your personal prayer for your child(ren):

_____
_____
_____
_____
_____
_____
_____
_____
_____
_____
_____
_____
_____
_____
_____
_____
_____
_____
_____
_____

**A Prayer Book for My Child(ren)**

## Gratitude and Acknowledgement:

Please write your reflections on your answered personal prayer:

_____
_____
_____
_____
_____
_____
_____
_____
_____
_____
_____
_____
_____
_____
_____
_____
_____
_____
_____
_____

# The Back/Spine

Exodus 1:9 (NIV) | The Lord will fight for you, you need only be still.

Lord, we thank You for blessing our child with a strong back that will enable him/her to stand strong. If your child has health challenges with their back/spine, we pray for miracles and swift healing.

We also pray he/she is aware that You will always be their strength. Please remind our child that when no one else is consistent or present, You are the one who is consistent, omnipotent, and all-knowing.

*For the Lord God is a sun and shield: the Lord will give grace and glory: no good thing will he withhold from them that walk uprightly.* **Psalms 84:11 (KJV)**

> **We pray the Lord will bless and protect our child's back and spine.**

Insert a Picture of _____ back/spine ☺
(Insert your child's name)

> This is your "Safe Space."
> Feel free to express yourself.

# In this moment:

What are your present thoughts, feelings, and emotions?

_____
_____
_____
_____
_____
_____
_____
_____
_____
_____
_____
_____
_____
_____
_____
_____

## In this moment:

Write your personal prayer for your child(ren):

_____
_____
_____
_____
_____
_____
_____
_____
_____
_____
_____
_____
_____
_____
_____
_____
_____
_____
_____
_____

## Gratitude and Acknowledgement:

Please write your reflections on your answered personal prayer:

_____
_____
_____
_____
_____
_____
_____
_____
_____
_____
_____
_____
_____
_____
_____
_____
_____
_____
_____
_____
_____
_____
_____

# The Hands

Psalm 24:4-5 (KJV) | He that hath clean hands, and a pure heart; who hath not lifted up his soul, unto vanity nor sworn deceitfully. He shall receive the blessing from the God of his salvation.

Lord, we thank you for giving our child hands. If your child has health challenges with their hands, we pray for miracles and that they will be healed soon. We pray that with these hands, he/she will build and develop great things. We also pray that our child will use them in prayer (*always using them in a positive manner to clap, praise, and function in life*). Please help keep our child from danger, out of trouble, and from falling into the wrong hands. Lastly, we pray that you will hold their hand as they mature in life.

*Thou will show me the path of life; in thy presence is full of joy at thy right hand there are pleasures forevermore.*
**Psalms 16:11 (NKJV)**

> **We pray the Lord will bless and protect our child's hands.**

Insert a Picture of _____ hands ☺
(Insert your child's name)

**A Prayer Book for My Child(ren)**

> This is your "Safe Space."
> Feel free to express yourself.

# In this moment:

What are your present thoughts, feelings, and emotions?

_____
_____
_____
_____
_____
_____
_____
_____
_____
_____
_____
_____
_____
_____
_____
_____
_____
_____
_____
_____

## In this moment:

Write your personal prayer for your child(ren):

_____
_____
_____
_____
_____
_____
_____
_____
_____
_____
_____
_____
_____
_____
_____
_____
_____
_____
_____
_____

# Gratitude and Acknowledgement:

Please write your reflections on your answered personal prayer:

_____
_____
_____
_____
_____
_____
_____
_____
_____
_____
_____
_____
_____
_____
_____
_____
_____
_____

# The Arms

Mark 10:16 (KJV) | And he took them up in his arms, put his hands upon them, and blessed them.

Lord, we thank you for blessing our child with a strong arm. We pray they can effectively carry out their day-to-day tasks using the strength of their arms.

God, grant our child strength in their arms to lift, move and change. We hope our child(ren) will praise you by raising their arms and showing love. We also pray they love themselves unconditionally. Lastly, please help them reach and offer help to others (*when they are capable*).

*The Lord is my strength and song and he is become my salvation: he is my God and I will prepare Him a habitation; my father's God and I will exhalt him.* **Exodus 15:2 (KJV)**

> **We pray the Lord will bless,
> protect and strengthen our child's arms.**

Insert a Picture of _____ arms ☺
(Insert your child's name)

A Prayer Book for My Child(ren)

> This is your "Safe Space."
> Feel free to express yourself.

## In this moment:

What are your present thoughts, feelings, and emotions?

_____
_____
_____
_____
_____
_____
_____
_____
_____
_____
_____
_____
_____
_____
_____
_____

# In this moment:

Write your personal prayer for your child(ren):

_____
_____
_____
_____
_____
_____
_____
_____
_____
_____
_____
_____
_____
_____
_____
_____
_____
_____
_____
_____

## Gratitude and Acknowledgement:

Please write your reflections on your answered personal prayer:

# The Belly

Job 40:16 (KJV) | Lo now, his strength is in his loins, and his force is in the navel of his belly.

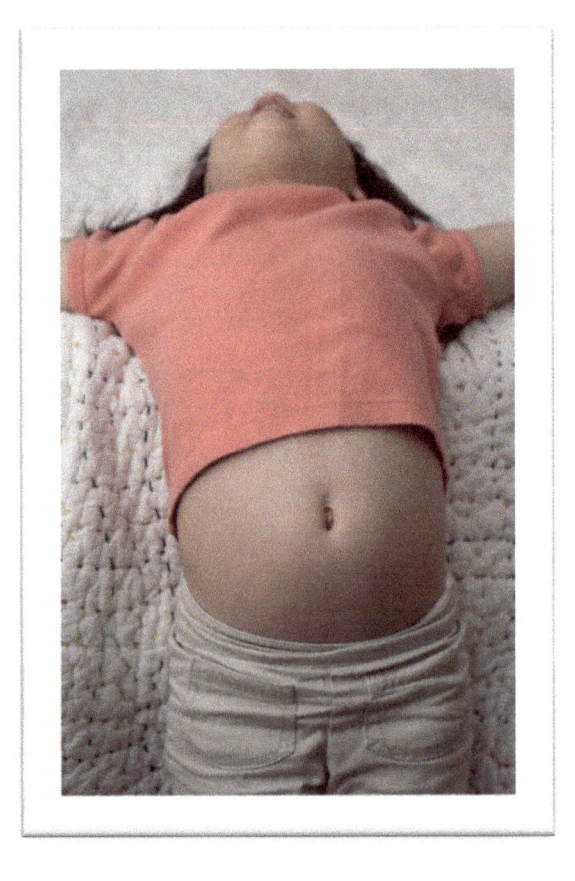

Lord, we thank You for blessing our child with a belly/stomach that is present to help him/her survive. If your child has health challenges with their stomach or internal organs, we pray for miracles and that they will be healed soon. We pray they can always digest and process food properly. We also pray You would dive deep into their belly and fill them with your truth, spirit, love, and kindness. Gird them up with the strength which stems from their navel. Help our child to believe in You starting now from the depths of their belly and outward. Out of their belly shall flow rivers of living water.

Lord, we pray You continue to protect our child's stomach/belly area so they can live a healthy life. We also pray that You help them make good choices regarding what they place in their belly so they may live a long God-filled life.

*The spirit of man is the candle of the LORD, searching all the inward parts of the belly.* **Proverbs 20:27 (KJV)**

*He that believeth on me, as the scripture hath said, out of his belly shall flow rivers of living water.* **John 7:38 (KJV)**

> **We pray the Lord will bless, protect and strengthen our child's belly.**

Insert a Picture of _____ belly ☺
(Insert your child's name)

**A Prayer Book for My Child(ren)**

> This is your "Safe Space."
> Feel free to express yourself.

# *In this moment:*

What are your present thoughts, feelings, and emotions?

_____
_____
_____
_____
_____
_____
_____
_____
_____
_____
_____
_____
_____
_____
_____
_____
_____
_____

## In this moment:

Write your personal prayer for your child(ren):

_____
_____
_____
_____
_____
_____
_____
_____
_____
_____
_____
_____
_____
_____
_____
_____
_____
_____
_____
_____

## Gratitude and Acknowledgement:

Please write your reflections on your answered personal prayer:

_____
_____
_____
_____
_____
_____
_____
_____
_____
_____
_____
_____
_____
_____
_____
_____
_____
_____
_____

# The Heart

Matthew 5:8 (KJV) | Blessed are the pure in heart: for they shall see God.

Lord, we thank You for blessing our child with a heart. If your child has health challenges with their heart, we pray for miracles and that they will be healed soon. The heart is the organ that beats and pulsates to allow life throughout his/her entire body. We pray You will continue to strengthen the hearts of our children. We also pray You would clean their heart so that it is pure and filled with the fruits of the spirit. Fill it with Your purity, truth, spirit, love, and kindness.

Lord, we pray You continue to protect our child's heart so they can live a healthy life. We also pray You'll help them as they learn to make proper choices. Please guide them always and in all ways.

*Let us draw near with a true heart in full assurance of faith, having our hearts sprinkled from an evil conscience, and our bodies washed with pure water.* **Hebrews 10:22 (KJV)**

*Blessed are they that keep his testimonies, and that seek him with the whole heart.* **Psalms 119:2 (KJV)**

> **We pray the Lord will bless, protect and strengthen our child's heart.**

Insert a Picture of _____ heart area ☺
(Insert your child's name)

**A Prayer Book for My Child(ren)**

> This is your "Safe Space."
> Feel free to express yourself.

# In this moment:

What are your present thoughts, feelings, and emotions?

_____
_____
_____
_____
_____
_____
_____
_____
_____
_____
_____
_____
_____
_____
_____
_____
_____

# In this moment:

Write your personal prayer for your child(ren):

_____

_____

_____

_____

_____

_____

_____

_____

_____

_____

_____

_____

_____

_____

_____

_____

_____

**A Prayer Book for My Child(ren)**

## Gratitude and Acknowledgement:

Please write your reflections on your answered personal prayer:

# The Private & Sacred Area

1 Timothy 5:22 (KJV) | Lay hands suddenly on no man, neither be partaker of other men's sins: keep thyself pure.

## Do Not Touch...

Lord, we thank You for blessing our child with a sacred area that will eventually allow him/her to procreate. We hope You will give them the strength and self-discipline to wait until they are married (to engage in marital activities). If your child has health challenges with their private/sacred area, we pray for miracles and that they will be healed soon.

Lord, we pray You continue to protect his/her sacred area so they are free from harm and misuse by anyone. We also pray they learn to be responsible and treat their bodies as temples.

*Marriage is honorable in all, and the bed undefiled: but whoremongers and adulterers God will judge.*
**Hebrews 13:4 (KJV)**

*Lo now, his strength is in his loins, and his force is in the navel of his belly.* **Job 40:16 (KJV)**

*Flee also youthful lusts: but follow righteousness, faith, charity, peace, with them that call on the Lord out of a pure heart.* **2 Timothy 2:22 (KJV)**

*Blessed are the undefiled in the way, who walk in the law of the LORD.* **Psalms 119:1 (KJV)**

*Know ye not that ye are the temple of God, and that the spirit of God dwelleth in you.* **Corinthians 3:16 (KJV)**

> **We pray the Lord will bless, protect and strengthen our child's private parts.**

Insert a picture of you embracing your child! ☺

**A Prayer Book for My Child(ren)**

> This is your "Safe Space."
> Feel free to express yourself.

# In this moment:

What are your present thoughts, feelings, and emotions?

_____
_____
_____
_____
_____
_____
_____
_____
_____
_____
_____
_____
_____
_____
_____
_____
_____

## In this moment:

Write your personal prayer for your child(ren):

_____
_____
_____
_____
_____
_____
_____
_____
_____
_____
_____
_____
_____
_____
_____
_____
_____
_____
_____
_____
_____
_____
_____
_____

## Gratitude and Acknowledgement:

Please write your reflections on your answered personal prayer:

# The Legs

Song of Solomon 5:15 (KJV)| His legs are as pillars of marble, set upon sockets of fine gold: his countenance is as Lebanon, excellent as the cedars.

Lord, we thank You for healthy, strong legs that will carry our son/daughter all the days of his/her life. We hope he/she will develop and You will protect their legs. Also, I pray that they will use their leg strength to accomplish positive things in life when they are able. If your child has health challenges with their legs/thighs/glutes, we pray for miracles and that they will be healed soon.

We pray that when he/she is able, they will use their leg strength to do positive things in life. If our child participates in sports, please give them the strength and perseverance to endure. Please lead them and guide them in your direction Lord.

*His legs of iron, his feet part of iron and part of clay.*
**Daniel 2:33 (KJV)**

*But they that wait upon the LORD shall renew their strength; they shall mount up with wings as eagles; they shall run, and not be weary; and they shall walk, and not faint.*
**Isaiah 40:31 (KJV)**

> **We pray the Lord will bless, protect and strengthen our child's legs.**

Insert a picture of _____ legs ☺
(Insert your child's name)

**A Prayer Book for My Child(ren)**

> **This is your "Safe Space."**
> **Feel free to express yourself.**

# In this moment:

What are your present thoughts, feelings, and emotions?

_____
_____
_____
_____
_____
_____
_____
_____
_____
_____
_____
_____
_____
_____
_____
_____

*In this moment:*

Write your personal prayer for your child(ren):

_____
_____
_____
_____
_____
_____
_____
_____
_____
_____
_____
_____
_____
_____
_____
_____
_____
_____
_____
_____

## Gratitude and Acknowledgement:

Please write your reflections on your answered personal prayer:

# The Knees

Luke 11:1 (KJV)| And it came to pass, that, as he was praying in a certain place, when he ceased, 1 of his disciples said until him Lord teach us to pray as John also taught his disciples.

Lord, I pray that his/her knees will sustain the weight of any experiences. If your child has health challenges with their knees, we pray for miracles and that they will be healed soon. I pray they will grow to understand that they should fall to their knees during prayer. I pray they will learn to repent and seek a divine relationship with You while being on their knees in prayer.

*But go ye and learn what that meaneth, I will have mercy, and not sacrifice: for I am not come to call the righteous, but sinners to repentance.* **Matthew 9:13 (KJV)**

> **We pray the Lord will bless,
> protect and strengthen our child's knees.**

Insert a Picture of _____ knees ☺
(Insert your child's name)

> This is your "Safe Space."
> Feel free to express yourself.

## In this moment:

What are your present thoughts, feelings, and emotions?

_____
_____
_____
_____
_____
_____
_____
_____
_____
_____
_____
_____
_____
_____
_____
_____
_____
_____

## In this moment:

Write your personal prayer for your child(ren):

_____
_____
_____
_____
_____
_____
_____
_____
_____
_____
_____
_____
_____
_____
_____
_____
_____
_____
_____
_____

**A Prayer Book for My Child(ren)**

# Gratitude and Acknowledgement:

Please write your reflections on your answered personal prayer:

_____
_____
_____
_____
_____
_____
_____
_____
_____
_____
_____
_____
_____
_____
_____
_____
_____
_____
_____

# The Feet

2 Samuel 22:37 (KJV)| Thou hast enlarged my steps under me; so that my feet did not slip.

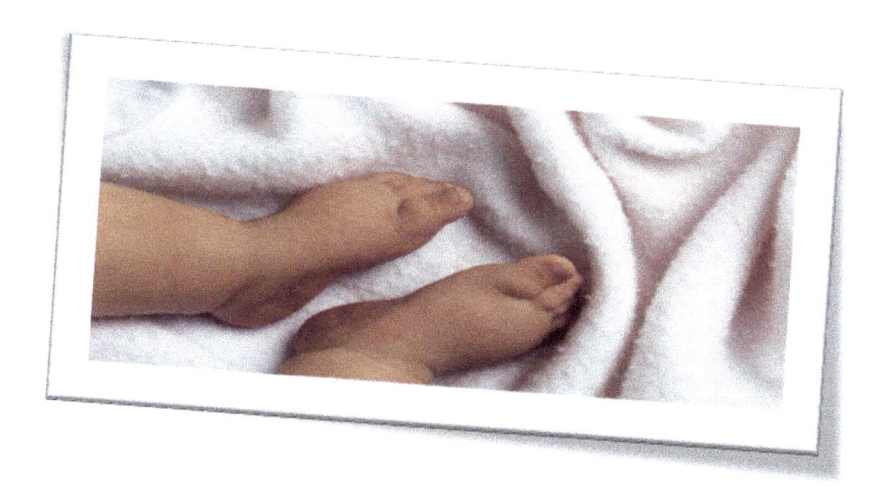

L ord, we thank You for our son's/daughter's feet and toes. If your child has health challenges with their feet, we pray for miracles and that they will be healed soon. We pray You allow them to function as they should throughout their life. We also pray You will lead them down the paths which will enable them to live out their purpose, as they walk with You. Once our child is planted, please help them to stay close to You.

*He maketh my feet like hind's feet setteth me upon my high places.* **2 Samuel 22:34 (KJV)**

*The steps of a good man are ordered by the LORD: and he delighteth in his way.* **Psalm 33:33 (KJV)**

*Order my steps in thy word; and let not any iniquity have dominion over me.* **Psalm 119:133 (KJV)**

> **We pray the Lord will bless,
> protect and strengthen our child's feet.**

Insert a Picture of _____ feet ☺
(Insert your child's name)

A Prayer Book for My Child(ren)

> This is your "Safe Space."
> Feel free to express yourself.

# In this moment:

What are your present thoughts, feelings, and emotions?

_____
_____
_____
_____
_____
_____
_____
_____
_____
_____
_____
_____
_____
_____
_____
_____
_____
_____

*In this moment:*

Write your personal prayer for your child(ren):

_____
_____
_____
_____
_____
_____
_____
_____
_____
_____
_____
_____
_____
_____
_____
_____
_____
_____
_____

**A Prayer Book for My Child(ren)**

# Gratitude and Acknowledgement:

Please write your reflections on your answered personal prayer:

# You

Malachi 4:2 (KJV)| But unto you that fear my name shall the Sun of righteousness arise with healing in his wings; and ye shall go forth, and grow up as calves of the stall.

Lord, thank You for planning and allowing each and every area of our son's/daughter's body to work and function as You see fit. If there are illnesses, ailments, handicaps, broken bones, etc., I pray You will heal only as you know how. I pray for increased faith for the parents & caregivers. Their faith is necessary, and so is your healing power!

*And the people, when they knew it, followed him: and he received them, and spoke unto them of the kingdom of God, and healed them that had need of healing.* **Luke 9:11 (KJV)**

*In the midst of the street of it, and on either side of the river, was there the tree of life, which bare twelve manner of fruits, and yielded her fruit every month: and the leaves of the tree were for the healing of the nations.*
**Revelation 22:2 (KJV)**

**Amen, Amen and Amen!!!**

> This is your "Safe Space."
> Feel free to express yourself.

## In this moment:

What are your present thoughts, feelings, and emotions?

_____
_____
_____
_____
_____
_____
_____
_____
_____
_____
_____
_____
_____
_____
_____
_____
_____
_____
_____

## In this moment:

Write your personal prayer for your child(ren):

**A Prayer Book for My Child(ren)**

## Gratitude and Acknowledgement:

Please write your reflections on your answered personal prayer:

_____
_____
_____
_____
_____
_____
_____
_____
_____
_____
_____
_____
_____
_____
_____
_____
_____
_____
_____
_____

Insert a picture of your family! ☺

**A Prayer Book for My Child(ren)**

*Write a Special Prayer* for you and your family! ☺

_____
_____
_____
_____
_____
_____
_____
_____
_____
_____
_____
_____
_____
_____
_____
_____
_____
_____
_____
_____
_____
_____

**A Prayer Book for My Child(ren)**

*Write something* you received from this book

(ex: peace, understanding, comfort….)

_____
_____
_____
_____
_____
_____
_____
_____
_____
_____
_____
_____
_____
_____

# Reflections and Feelings

and Yes, Your Child needs Prayer too:

_____
_____
_____
_____
_____
_____
_____
_____
_____
_____
_____
_____
_____
_____
_____
_____
_____
_____
_____
_____
_____
_____

**A Prayer Book for My Child(ren)**

## Personal Notes,

Ideas, thoughts & prayers you may have……

_____
_____
_____
_____
_____
_____
_____
_____
_____
_____
_____
_____

Personal Notes, Ideas, thoughts & prayers you may have cont'd

_____
_____
_____
_____
_____
_____
_____
_____
_____
_____
_____
_____
_____
_____
_____
_____
_____
_____
_____
_____
_____
_____
_____
_____
_____
_____

**A Prayer Book for My Child(ren)**

Personal Notes, Ideas, thoughts & prayers you may have cont'd

**A Prayer Book for My Child(ren)**

Personal Notes, Ideas, thoughts & prayers you may have cont'd

_____
_____
_____
_____
_____
_____
_____
_____
_____
_____
_____
_____
_____
_____
_____
_____
_____
_____
_____
_____
_____

**A Prayer Book for My Child(ren)**

## Personal Notes, Ideas, thoughts & prayers you may have cont'd

_____
_____
_____
_____
_____
_____
_____
_____
_____
_____
_____
_____
_____
_____
_____
_____
_____
_____
_____
_____
_____
_____
_____
_____
_____

**A Prayer Book for My Child(ren)**

Printed in the USA
CPSIA information can be obtained
at www.ICGtesting.com
JSHW071643150923
48171JS00014B/114

9 781953 163486